Contents

Say the sounds

j v w x y ch
sh th ng

Jim and Nan

Jim

I am Jim and this is my Nan.

Nan

She is my dad's mum.

A box of toys

Nan has a box of my dad's toys.

book

farm set

cars

4

Dad had this farm set long ago.

He was six then!

Toy cars

Can you see the red van?

My dad had lots of toy cars.

6

Books

This was Dad's best book.

Land of the giants

My book can pop up!

Rockets

My dad had this rocket.

Dad's rocket

He was seven then!

Look at my rocket!

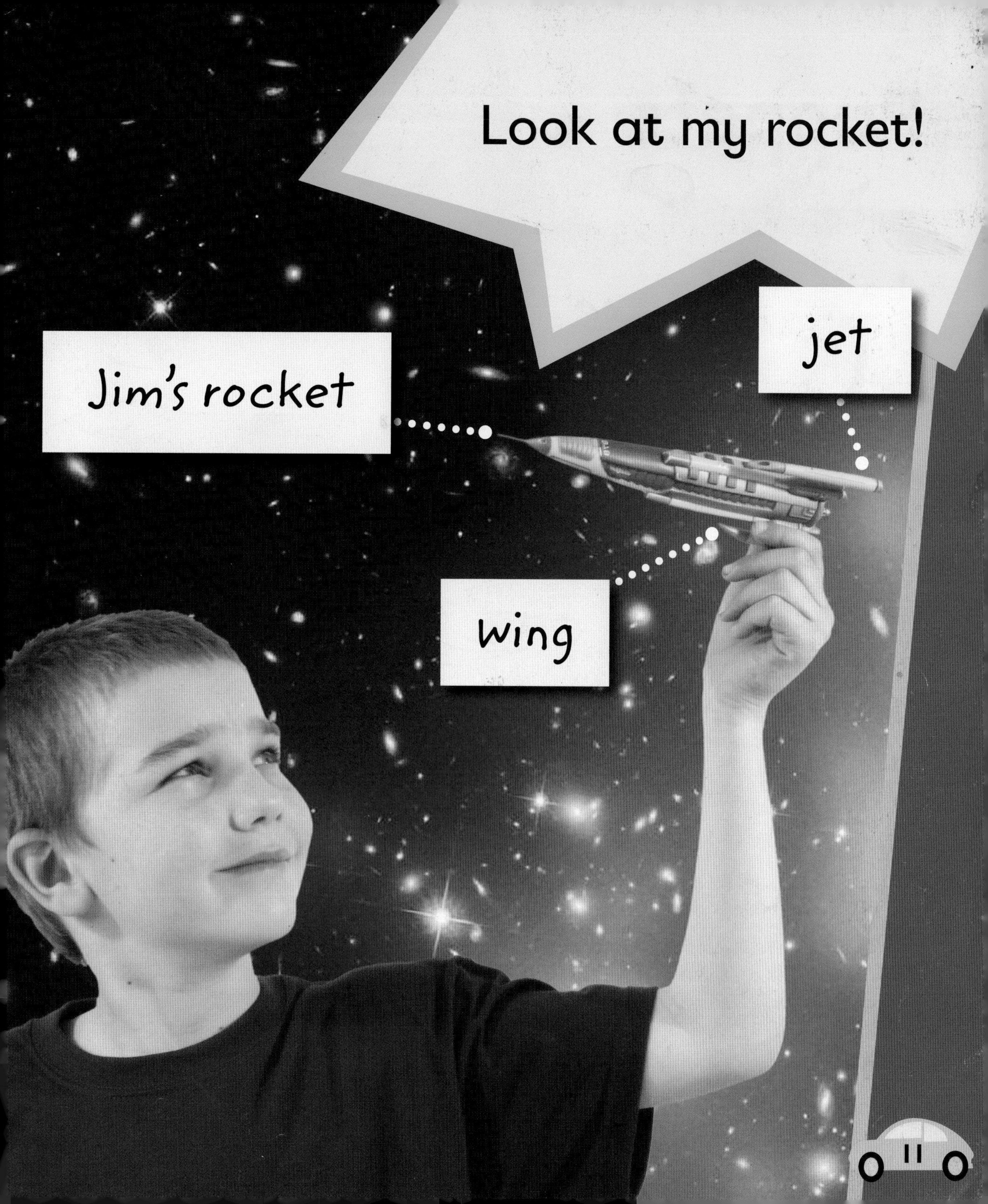

Puppets

Dad had this puppet.

My puppet is fun too!

Best toys

This was my
dad's model ship.

It was his best toy.

15

Index